ARCHIVIST *of* ALMOSTS

NATASHA RAHMAN KHAN

Archivist of Almosts

ISBN 978-93-344-2245-0
First Edition

For my mother, who believed in this book.
And for those who wander pages to feel a little less alone.

NOTE FROM THE ARCHIVIST

I have been followed by shadows
longer than I can remember.
And I definitely did not set out to write a book.

But poetry has a way of catching up
when I spend years running from reflections
that looked too much like grief—
too much like me.
I tried to outpace them, outgrow them,
but they always found me,
in the pause between metaphors in my brain.

And somewhere between wanting to write the stanza and the scar,
I found a pulse.

It whispered memories I had tried to bury.
It pointed at locked doors I had painted over.
It asked nothing but honesty.

So, I turned to face the shadow at last,
and it gave me a pen.

...

This book is a collection of poetry I scribbled over the years. It will take you through childhood, connections, the lost and found, the pain that eats you whole, the ghosts that linger in your head, and rooms that don't exactly want to let go. Within these pages, you are not solitary.

Every step you take, I've taken.
Every silence you hold, I have heard.
Come, let me walk you through.

THE ARCHIVE

Welcome to the Archive.
Catalogued by: The Archivist.
Access Level: Authorized Entry.
Date Opened: ____________
Keyholder Identified: ____________
Key Code: [redacted]

...

...

>>> Six rooms have been restored.

...

[Enter]

ARCHIVE CATALOG

Room 1— Of Petals and Roots

Room 2— Of Graves and Return

Room 3— Of Anchors and Ink

Status: Stained and Intact

Memory Type: Love-Locked Relics

Room 4— Of Survivors and Storms

Status: Fragile

Memory Type: War-Torn Pages

Room 5— Of Sinners and Sin

Status: Restricted (Red Seal)

Memory Type: Moral Transcripts

Archivist Notes:

"Some summers don't end—
they linger where the wind last laughed."

"Of Petals And Roots"

ROOM No.: 1
Observer Type: For the Dreamers
Status: Unsealed
Memory Type: Early Echoes
Lighting Condition: Golden hour glow
Compiled By: The Archivist
Date Restored: [redacted]

THE POET AND THE PERIWINKLE

I've always wondered who gave me my poetic side.

Mid-June,
late afternoons always looked
and landed like a lingering,
gentle glide back,
even when the bare beginning
of the year felt unbalanced.

Today, a breezy, bold, childish
giggle rode on the rising wind,
nudging the open window,
pushing playful puffs of air inside
and whispering,

"May I come in?"

My silent signal sufficed.
He surged through the soft sheets of curtain—
a shouting, satisfied *"Here I am!"* trailing in his wake.

Clothes, long forgotten, tumbled from their hooks,
collapsing into soft heaps of laughter on the floor
as he danced all around his new-found space.

The periwinkle's pretty petals at the sill
pulsed in perfect parallel, swaying to his song.
The room itself drew a deep breath,
the walls rising like living lungs,

while the ceiling's churning fan thrummed a tender roar,
caught in the clear, chaotic call of his joyful journey.

The wind, my wanderer friend, finally flies home,
whispering worlds of wild tales against my petals.
He spins, jubilant, to find me rooted—
still here, yet blossomed bolder.

His current halts, awestruck by my five-petaled bloom.
He swirls me into his dance,
his invisible hand tugging at the poet's heart,
drawing her to my side.

She settles close, her presence a quiet comfort.
Then, the gentle lift of her fingers—
to her mother, she speaks of my loveliness.
I blush, a deeper pink pulsing through my purple.

A sweet curve of her lips,
the lightest touch—
a breath of a kiss lands softly against my bloom.

Back at my desk, the work lay untouched.
My eyes, instead, kept drifting
toward the window's edge
to that one periwinkle.

The wind danced around it,
but the branch leaned in, deliberate,

as if remembering a room, it once loved.

“Mom, look!” I pointed. “It’s trying to come inside.”
She followed my gaze, a smile blooming across her face.
“You touched it with kindness,” she said.
“It’s reaching right *back for you.”*

And in that moment— that still, tender moment,
her words stirred something quiet but certain in me.
Not a new knowing,
but an old one returning home.

My mother.
Of course.
The root of the rhythm.
The first metaphor.
The breath beneath every blooming word I’ve ever written.

“Poets,” I shook my head, laughing.
They do find the grandest poems in the smallest whispers, don’t they?

THE WIND REMEMBERS

The wind met me *first—*
a sudden gust,
dusty, fragrant, insistent.
It pressed into me like an old friend,
carrying songs I thought I'd lost:
the ice-cream man's tinny jingle,
the sharp, sweet breath of wet clay,
the laughter of cousins
still bright with afternoon sun.

Where I come from, the city is hardened
into layers of cement and stone.
But here, the heavens hung
vast, dreamy, present,
and *protective.*
Time toiled no tricks but took a tender truce,
a world away from the constant city's clamor,
where dreamers drown in dull smoke
and hard, heavy horizons.

A single, soaring shade of yellow
tore the tapestry of the twin horizons.
A kite—
and *a girl* beneath it.
With her laughter braided into its string,
her small hand steady against the pull of the sky.

I knew that shade.
It was the one you once clutched,
close against your chest,
refusing to let its string slip.

The wind pressed harder,
blowing open a door I hadn't meant to knock on.
And I was pulled into a perfect past.
And there you were...
small, barefoot, hair ungoverned by combs—
a little girl with a yellow kite.

You were the quiet strength
in a noisy storm of cousins,
the first hand steady on the string,
the first to leap when others faltered.
Your sure grip guided everyone,
skimming the sea of fields
toward the river we *"sailors"*
had decided to sail that day.

We had spied a slumbering,
abandoned boat by the river, and finally,
on that thrilling day, we'd take the plunge.

We imagined ourselves in mighty oceans,
fighting fierce waves.
None knew how to row,
and the oar was missing,
not that we searched—
for what use was rowing
to sailors who believed the river obeyed them?

But then the boat, a still, silent shell
seemed to shift beneath us.

Water pooled in,

and our shoes sank, soaked.
A hole in the boat revealed itself.

Then, one seafaring sailor shouted:
"The ship is wrecked by a mighty sea-monster!"
Our imaginations took over—
wild with the thrill of escape.

In truth, the water was calm, barely shallow.
But imagination was *our element.*
And again, you were the support.

You guided everyone out,
carrying the youngest, helping the smallest.
To this day, we cousins still cherish
that tale of the sailors.

You were fearless then.
And I almost envy you now,
the way you used to run barefoot into storms,
calling danger by its first name.

And for a moment,
I stood outside your life,
older eyes tracing younger limbs,
as though I were both subject and spectator,
both watched and watcher.

The wind still pressed, whispering,
reminding, returning.

Then, just beyond the horizon of memory,
a new present emerged.
A field full of children danced with colour,
their kites turning the sky into a canvas of dreams.

Each string stretched like a lifeline into joy,

each colour a call to childhood.
I stood still, watching,
when I felt a tug on my hand.
I looked down.

The girl with the yellow kite stood there,
like a memory I was meant to find.
Her smile split the silence.
Her eyes held galaxies—
not the kind above,
but the kind within.

"Come, join us?" she asked.

Her voice carried echoes of every summer past,
of every name I had ever answered to
before I became an adult.

And just like that,
the years unbuttoned themselves
and slipped away.

My hand, now small again,
looked perfectly like hers.
And I knew her—
the way one knows oneself in a mirror.
The *"you"* I had chased across fields,
the girl with dreams in her pockets,
was me.

And I ran...
barefoot,
into the field,
into the sky,
into the wind
that had always been
waiting for me.

Archivist Notes:

"They don't all stay buried..."

"Of Graves And Return"

ROOM No.: 2
Observer Type: For the Wanderers
Status: Partially Disturbed
Memory Type: Residual Hauntings
Lighting Condition: Low lamplight; cold
Compiled By: The Archivist
Date Restored: [redacted]

NOT ALL GHOSTS SLAM DOORS

They said she hanged herself in the kitchen.
That she'd been told to marry a man she didn't love, and
when the house fell silent one evening,
she climbed onto something tall
and left the world with no witnesses.

But I remember her differently.
Every time I came back to the village,
she'd sit cross-legged next to me,
listening to my stories from the city.

She lived next door to my grandfather's house.
Same age as me.
She had eyes that dreamed even when they blinked,
and a voice that always ended in a soft upward lilt—
like a question left open.

She was the kind of girl who believed in more.
More sky. More love. More *time.*
Her dreams were always just one window too high.

As we grew up, her family cared for my grandmother.
She became her quiet, constant support.
And when my grandmother passed,
the house changed,
but she stayed on.
Some ties don't need legal threads to hold.

Grief settled quietly in the house,
but the girl's story remained unspoken.
No one said *"suicide,"*
not at first.
Only later,
at the burial,
did whispers slip between adults:
someone had noticed the marks.

I still remember the hush of that burial.
Rumors settled in like dust:
It was her *own* scarf.
It was heartbreak.
It was *rebellion.*
It was *the kitchen.*

And with those whispers,
the house changed again.
They say it's haunted now.
They said she didn't scream.
They said her sister found her first
and never cooked in that room again.

When we were children,
we shared mango slices and stories.
When we were older,
we shared struggles and secrets.

And when she was gone,
truly gone—
I didn't cry,
not right away.
The grief came in pieces.

Some swore they saw her
out of the corner of their eye,
or felt her breath behind them

when no one was there.

Years after the burial, I sat there alone,
and it felt like stepping into a story she left unfinished.
I spoke aloud, hoping she was there.

The walls held a breath.
Almost like she was sitting with me again, listening.
Time slowed down enough to feel grief inch by inch.

And I sat there,
staring at the tiles,
anger climbing my throat.

I had more stories to tell you—
you had more stories to listen to.
I came back every summer.
I was your friend.
If no one else heard you, you knew *I* would have.

Why didn't you tell me?
Why didn't you trust me with your pain?
Why did you leave me with rumors and silence,
leave me to imagine the knot, the scarf,
in the empty room that swallowed you whole?
You let whispers carry what your *voice* should have.

The questions burned holes into the stillness.
And in that stillness, I felt it—
a weight pressing soft against my chest,
as if the air itself bent close enough
to mouth the one thing that she never said.

"Sorry."
A hollow apology.

Not all ghosts slam doors.

Some just stay in rooms
where they were last heard.
They linger quietly,
their lives folded away
like clothes they can no longer wear,
their things scattered
like unspoken prayers.

Meanwhile we,
the ones left behind,
beg the silence for *another chance,*
another word,
another summer—
anything to guide them home,
anything to make them stay,
anything to not be so late.

THE PAINTING

Lately I begin to wonder
if some paintings don't preserve faces,
but trap them.

It was always the girl in the middle,
the smallest of the three,
whose candle never seemed to go out.

They said it was just a painting.
Three sisters, three candles,
one frame too still to stir.

But every time I entered that dusky room,
where silence danced like quiet spirits in light-slits,
it was her eyes I met first.

And her candle?
Still glowing, even in the dark.

The teachers chalked it up to reflective paint.
But even science can't explain
why she followed you with her eyes.
or why the air inside that room always felt...
one breath too full.

But I was a child.
And when you're a child,
mystery is your mother tongue.

I used to stare at that portrait during class,
half-listening to animations,
half-hoping she'd blink.
She never moved, but somehow,
she never stayed *still.*

Then came the evening.
It was just me and a friend
in the main hall above the room,
the sky outside slipping fast into indigo.

The teacher had left.
We practiced our steps, carefree,
until the music started again—
unprovoked.

The same song,
pressing play on its own.
We brushed it off.
We were used to strange things.

But when I was alone,
laces untied,
speaker in hand,
hallway quiet,
I passed the room.

Something darted past the frosted glass.
A shape, a shift— quick and deliberate.
I stopped. Peered in.

I opened the door.
The room was dark, but not empty.

Not truly.

Her candle still burned.
And for the first time, I thought it *flickered.*
Soft, like a breath.

I stood there longer than I meant to.
Something about the air—
thick, velvet-dark,
pressed against my skin
like a breath held too long.

I didn't move until
the hallway light behind me flickered once,
then stilled.

I backed away, slowly,
as though disturbing something ancient,
something brittle.

My shoes barely touched the floor,
but every step felt heard.
Known.
Followed.

The door creaked closed behind me,
with a sigh.
Like it was letting me go...
just this once.

Behind me, my friend called my name
from the far end of the hallway.
Her voice was distant, familiar,
calling me back to where things made sense.

By the time I reached her,
her face was bright with chatter,

unaware of the hush I carried with me,
a hush that clung like cobweb.

I said nothing.
What could *I say?*
That the painting had *looked back?*
That the candle *might breathe?*

That night, I dreamt of a terrace that no longer exists.
Empty sky, broken laughter, a fall no one saw
but everyone remembers.

They say her sisters didn't mean to push her.
That it was...
an accident.

Adults dismissed it all, said it was just a story.
But stories don't settle in bones unless
something lets them *in.*

Years later, I returned for a school reunion.
Just to meet some teachers,
I stayed back after school hours again.
I found myself in front of the glass door.

Empty corridor. Same door. Same silence.
They'd renovated the room, stripped the walls,
but the painting was still there.
I paused at the threshold,
half-expecting her candle to blink back into being.

You know, there are some things you leave behind,
and others, that wait where you left them.
And memory?
It's just a room you sometimes still pass,
where the light flickers
for no reason at all.

Even now, years later,
in old buildings, forgotten hallways,
or quiet Sunday evenings—
I still pause.
Somewhere in me,
a girl with wide eyes and a candle still waits,
her flame shifting subtly when they look away,
watching, always, from the frame I never left.

WHEN THE DEAD DIALS BACK

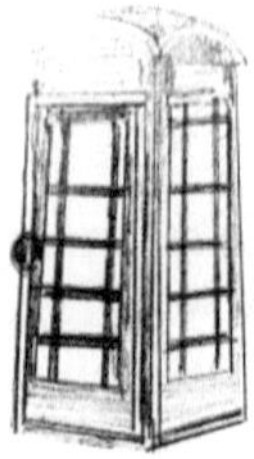

The booth stands where it always did...chipped paint, rust on the handle, glass smeared with old rain. ***Ninth Street*** is empty this time of night, but I still look both ways before stepping in.
The city sleeps, but some places remember.

The air inside is colder. Always colder.

I drop a coin.
The dial spins.
Static crackles. Then comes the tone.
I press the receiver to my ear.
"Hello?"

My own voice echoes back. And then...
a flicker.
A sigh that's not mine.
Faint. Familiar.
"There you are," I whisper, as if you'd been hiding just beyond the dial tone.

"You always take the long way back," you say.

Your voice carries that same crooked smile it always did.
But it shouldn't be here.

You shouldn't be here.
I watched them lower your body last winter.

"I thought maybe..." I pause.
"I thought maybe this time I wouldn't hear you."
Silence.
Then static stirs again.

"It's only been a day, love."

"No. It's been a year."
(Time collapses between us; the line hums louder.)

"You sound far away," I say.

"I am."

You laugh— soft and *wrong.*
Like the memory of a laugh told secondhand.

The line bends. The words stretch, slur. I hear another breath... this one harsh, metallic.

"I keep calling."

"I know."

"Why do you still answer?"
But you don't.

Instead, there's the clink of metal.
A knock. I don't look.
The sound of footsteps outside the booth follows,
And this time I turn, the street is still empty.

The air inside the booth chills.
The receiver hisses like something breathing between

the wires.

I close my eyes. I have my fair share of hauntings, it's alright to have one more. *It waits for me, as I wait for it.*

"You left without saying goodbye," I say.

"I thought if I didn't say it, it wouldn't stick."

"You're dead."

A pause.

I try to remember that day. The last time we saw each other in flesh and warmth. You wore that scarf I once called ridiculous— the red one with tiny flowers.
We sat on the old train platform, legs dangling,
talking about futures like they were easily built.
You leaned your head on my shoulder.
The wind was chilly.
The air was thick with soft dust and unsaid farewells.

We used to write letters too, remember?
Ink on torn pages, folded like secrets.
I'd wait by the gate, watching the postman's hands.
Even now, I think of your last one... the handwriting smaller than usual.

You said you'd miss my voice.
You said, *Speak often. Speak soft. I'll always be listening.*

The phone cord coils around my fingers like a promise.

"Do you remember what you told me last?"
You breathe in and then say:

"If I ever go quiet, don't follow the silence."

But I did.

Now the wires remember you better than I do.
The line clicks and the booth is quiet again.
I check the time.
It's later than I thought.

The street outside looks a little older.
The floor is littered with old bus tickets and a torn corner of a phone book.

My breath fogs the glass as I wait, not for the line to return,
but for the weight in my chest to settle.

Out on the street, the sodium lights flicker, then hold—unnaturally still.

A dog's bark cuts off mid-howl.
Then I hear it again: the faint sound of the line clicking.

Once.
Twice.

Like someone dialing *back in.* But no one else is here.
Then a radio hums to life somewhere too close,
a violin tune, warped and dragging like it's been playing for too long.
It scratches something in me I don't remember giving away.

I know this song.
You once hummed it when you thought I was asleep.
But you're not supposed to remember me anymore.
You're not supposed to answer back.

The receiver twitches slightly in its cradle. Like it's about to speak without me.
I don't touch it.

I reach for the door.
It opens on the second try.

I left the booth. But I don't think it let me go.
Some things don't release you so easily.

They say the dead don't speak.
I say: ***listen closer.***

3:47

The ticket bled through my palm like damp ink. No name for the station, no hour of arrival. Just a smear of numbers where time should have been.

The train waited like a thing exiled from time—steel sinews groaning, windows weeping fog, a breathless hush between rust and rush.

I stepped inside.

I took the last compartment. Chose it for its quiet. Or maybe it chose me. One man sat by the window, watching the blur beyond the glass.

He didn't blink.

I didn't ask his name.
The silence between us felt *rehearsed.*

We passed places I couldn't name, towns drained of colour, signs missing letters like teeth.
Even my watch began to falter—
ticks thinning, thinning, echoing like a hesitant heart.
Time pulling back like a tide that didn't plan to return.

The train felt like it had been moving forever.
Then came a station.

One lamp flickering above a cracked platform. No announcements. No passengers.

Something in my chest leaned forward. My body followed.
I stepped out.

Behind me, the train exhaled...
that sigh old engines make
when they know you won't be back.

I turned to look.

The man was already there.
Standing at the far end. Unmoved. Unchanged.
I hadn't seen him *step down.*
I hadn't seen him move at all.

I don't know why I stood. Only that I had.
As if I'd stood here before. As if the platform had been waiting for me all along.

My watch stopped. Hands froze at
3:47. Again.
They always do.

The benches bowed, burdened by the weight of waiting. The timetable was blank, as if the future had run out of ink.

Even the crows perched above:
silent, stiff, their black eyes chasing nothing—
didn't blink.

That's when I saw it.

A suitcase slouched by the bench, like a memory too

tired to stand.
Leather peeled at the seams.
One handle hung by a thread.
A tag dangled, soft in the stale wind.

My name.
Not typed.
Not clean.
Written in a hand that almost looked like mine,
but trembled where mine wouldn't.

Like someone had tried to remember me
—and almost did.

I knelt.

That's when I felt it:
footsteps, dragging,
damp as prayer, heavy as guilt,
across the platform.
Too slow to be mine.
Too *sure to be a stranger's.*
Too *close.*

I turned.
The man stood closer now.

His coat unmoved by the wind.
His face too still to be alive.
He looked at me, not with eyes, but with the knowing of someone who's folded your name into more obituaries than birthdays.

He pointed at the suitcase.
I opened it.

Inside:

A newspaper scrap, soft and yellowed,
as if time had folded it too many times.
One column.

Obituaries.
All the obituaries blurred,
except *one name—*
sharp.
Recent.
Mine.

The ink hadn't dried yet.

Under the name, a time etched in *the* same ink: ***3:47***.
They said Death only knocks once. Mine came at 3:47.
The door just never closed.

I stood there,
suitcase at my feet.

The man stepped forward.
He held something in his hand—my watch.
Still stuck.
As if time itself held its breath. **3.47.**

He slipped it back into my palm and whispered,
"They never scream the first time.
Only when they realize it's not the first."

I opened my mouth to speak, but no words came out.

He was...
Not a man.
Not really.
Too still for that.
Too *constant.*
Too old.

His eyes weren't eyes.
They were
mirrors.

And in them…
me.
again.
again.
again.

The same coat.
Same shoes.
Same fear blooming behind my ribs.

He took a step back, toward the train.
And I followed.
Without question.
Without sound.

The train always comes.
The station always waits.
And Death— *he never forgets the way.*

Not when he wears your face.
Not when he waits for your hour.
Not when he hands you the ticket *next.*

THE FINAL RHYME

I was here *before* the breath was born,
Before the dusk, before the morn.
Before the first life was ever penned,
I was made the herald of mortal end.

I knock but once. They rarely hear.
Some laugh, some cry, some draw me *near*.
Some nod as if they always knew,
That I am old. That I am true.

I bear the clocks of flesh and bone.
Each ticking life, I mark as my own.
Each holds time— a breath, a name.
No two alike. *But all the same.*

The train arrives; it never strays,
The wheels lament in endless ways.
And when the doors begin to part,
I feel the hush behind the heart.

They step into the waiting gloom,
A soul unsure, a borrowed bloom.
I greet them not with prayer or song,
But with the truth they've known all along.

I give them what was theirs to keep,
The watch that stopped, *the final sleep*.
For I am the pause, the final rhyme.
I am the grave of fleeting time.

And every soul, they wear the fears
That I have seen *for years and years.*
They think they walk this path alone,
Yet every face *reflects my own.*

I ride the end of every tale,
Where minutes falter and hours pale
I return what life once stole—
The watch, the name, the face, ***the soul.***

Archivist Notes:

"To love is to mark — in verse, in vow, in vein."

"Of Anchors And Ink"

ROOM No.: 3
Observer Type: For the Lovers
Status: Stained and Intact
Memory Type: Love-locked Relics
Lighting Condition: Lamplight; salty air
Compiled By: The Archivist
Date Restored: [redacted]

IN VERSE

You laughed like water,
once simple,
now rippling with meanings
I never asked for.
Even the way you said my name
felt like a borrowed metaphor,
as if I'd stolen it
from a gentler poem.

Your silence rhymed too clean, too true
with all the loneliness I knew.
So I made it art—gave it a frame,
Gave weight and rhythm to your name.

Your footsteps down the hallway's bend
became a line I'd never end.
A half-built bridge, a fading beat,
half-promise held, half-sure retreat.

Your distance, dressed in serifed grace,
I wrote in fonts that knew their place.
Italicized your drifting tone,
Romanticized being left alone.
Each sigh, a stanza.
Each goodbye,
a verse too soft
to question *why*.

Even how you stood in doorways,
half in, half gone,
became a metaphor
for the way you loved me.

Barely.
But enough for me
to make it mean more
than it ever was meant to be.

You peeled oranges with your thumbs.
You left socks like lazy crumbs.
You kissed like commas—never done,
each "later" hinting at *someone*.
You said it smooth, with pauses planned,
like words alone could hold my hand.

You didn't stay, but still I swore,
to gild the silence, fix the door.
The one you left open, just enough
for hope to hang on to your bluff.

But poets grieve in measured lines.
We count our ghosts. We shape their signs.
We beg the past to hold its form,
to stay just long enough to warm.
We trap what fades inside the cage
of metaphor, of ink, of page.

It's tiring—this kind of love,
When all that's left fits just above
a line break, or a turning phrase,
a ghost that lives in lowercase.

Still, I write you. Still, you stay,
in every margin, day by day.
Because forgetting feels like sin;

like admitting you were never in
this life, this chest, this aching skin.

That perhaps, in the end,
all you were was ink,
And I, the fool, who didn't think
that art could lie, or hearts could trick
themselves with verses they believed could stick.

And maybe that's the poet's crime—
We hold too close. We rhyme. We rhyme.
We bind, we bend, we bleed in prose,
We dress our wounds in whispered oaths.

You echo now
in every verse,
Not breath,
but syllables and curse.

And when they ask,
"Did he love you back?"
— I fake a laugh, evade the fact,
And I flinch at what I know I lack.
Still, I say,
"Yes, of course."
Once again, I lie.
Softly.
Like it's still mine to deny.

So, I rewrite.
I reshape.
I retell.
I relive.

I rewrite
because you burned so beautifully,
and I'm still chasing

the warmth
in the ashes.

  Because a poet
  like me
never lets go.
We just refine the ache
until it sounds
like something beautiful.

  Something like *'you.'*

THE LIGHTHOUSE

There was a time
I thought I'd drown quiet.
Not with thunder,
but with slow forgetting,
a ship fading
into the blur between horizon and night.

Salt on my tongue
grief in my hull.
No map, no north,
just the ache of wandering forth.

And in the blur of tides and night,
a flicker appeared...
A light I didn't trust at first.
Too steady.
Too kind.
Too much like hope.

You didn't rescue me.
You never threw ropes
or called me home.
You just... stayed.
A flame on the far edge of ruin,
soft as dusk,

stubborn as stars.

And I?
I turned toward you.
Your light
felt like something I could survive.
And you welcomed me
as if I'd never been lost at all.

You,
who never asked me
to be whole before you came through.
You,
whose silence said,
"Here. Anchor, if you must."

I have known love like storms before—
wild, gasping,
leaving wreckage in its wake.
But you,
you were the first
to teach me love
could be a place to rest.
A warmth that did not burn.
A light that did not blind or test.

You didn't fix me.
You didn't try.
But I learned to float again
just by watching you shine.

And if I am softer now,
if I speak with fewer walls somehow,
know this:

It is because I saw a lighthouse *once,*
and it looked like you.

And it never asked me
to be anything
but *a ship worth guiding through.*

KISS ME LIKE JUDAS

Let them keep the clean goodbyes,
the quiet fades, the softened lies.
The kind that leaves with folded grace,
no trace of fire, no aftertaste.

I don't want soft endings.
Give me grief that bites and stays,
that stains the bed and warps the days.

Be cruel,
be unkind.
Let me lose my breath,
gasp on the air you left behind.

I want the ache with teeth and claws,
the kind that never needs a cause.
The break that splits the soul in two,
and carves the scream right out of you.

No dressed metaphors.
No tidy prose.
I want your love,
the way it breaks,
the way it goes.

You said you'd stay.
Then prove you lied.
And when you leave,
don't say goodbye.

Give me madness I can taste.
Give me silence I can chase.
Give me nights I cannot sleep,
and days that rot me
inch by inch.

If you must go,
then go like sin.
And make me want
to let you in.

And maybe, someday,
I'll crawl from the rubble
of who I was
and thank you
for tearing me apart
so completely
I had to begin again
as someone else.

But not today.

Today,
I want the wreckage raw and sweet.
I want the breaking
on repeat.

If you must go,
then go like this—
a curse, a fever,
a Judas kiss.

Let me bleed and call it fair.
If you ever loved me,
ruin me bare.

Archivist Notes:

"Why is there no medal for just making it through?"

"Of Survivors And Storms"

ROOM No.: 4
Observer Type: For the Endurers
Status: Fragile
Memory Type: War-Torn Pages
Lighting Condition: Emergency Glow
Compiled By: The Archivist
Date Restored: [redacted]

SURVIVOR'S GUILT

They say time waits for no one.
And I swear it shoved me aside.

I stood at the mouth of the escalator,
résumé trembling in my grip,
a stitched-up dream beneath my coat,
watching the world step on
like they were born with boarding passes.

They didn't stumble.
They didn't look back.
Just rose...
carried upward in smooth procession:
briefcases, weddings, milestones,
hair tousled by the breeze of momentum.

I blinked—
and they were already gone.

My foot hovered.
I hesitated once.
That's all it took.
And by the time I exhaled,
it was too late.

Now I'm still here,
gripping a crumpled ticket
they say no longer scans.

I watch them pass again each morning,
same faces, newer suits,
the ones who knew when to move.
They carry stories in their stride,
smiling like the future
was promised to them in writing.

Some days, I rehearse the step:
One-two, lean through, blend in.
But the metal teeth glint like laughter now,
and my shoes feel too small
for the kind of motion they demand—
too soaked in doubt to lift.

It's not envy.
Not exactly.
Not even bitterness.

It's mourning.
For the version of me that moved too slow.
For the second
that made a year bleed.

It's a question:
What did I miss?

And a quieter answer:
One step.
The wrong hesitation.
The right mistake.

A minute too late,
and the world rewrote itself

without me.

That's the thing no one tells you;
once motion leaves you,
you don't just catch up.
You carry the stillness.
You wear it like shame.

Even progress has a schedule.
And the world?
It doesn't stop to ask why you stayed behind.

But try to catch up,
and they will.
Where were you?
Why the gap?
Why didn't you keep pace?
Why your records gather dust?
Why your name stopped appearing
in rooms it used to belong to?

As if a detour
makes your compass less valid.
As if grief
should've filed a two-week notice.
As if collapse
was a lifestyle choice.

I want to scream:
I was surviving, damn it.
I was trying to stand
while the floor kept shifting.

But they just raise eyebrows.
Tuck my silence
into the *"not a good fit" pile.*

They don't want reasons.
They want regret.
As if I can gather all the debris of failure
and file it neatly
under *"miscellaneous setbacks."*

They want dates.
A narrative they can skim.
Something to hang a justification on
so they can nod and move on.

They want the story sterilized.
The wound
worded in past tense.

But I remember—
I was right *here.*
Watching the escalator rise.
Carrying the weight
of a single missed step
like a sentence I'm still serving.

What do I say?
That I stood in a burning building
while they *scribbled feedback*
on how fast I could run?

I'm done whittling my hurt
into something polite.
Tired of polishing silence
into answers that sound like ambition.

I am not your cautionary tale.
I am not a pause you get to audit.
I am still here.
Still burning.
And I owe no one

a reason for surviving out of sync.

I still try, though.
I show up
in shoes that blister,
with a smile stitched
from borrowed hope.

I still dream,
knowing they'll measure me
by what I didn't become,
not by the fire I crawled through
just to be here.

And so, these days, you'd find me
shrink the truth, shaving the wound,
wrapping the year I spent rebuilding
into a single, polite sentence.

To which they nod,
and move on.

And I'm left
holding the weight of survival
like a red mark
on a clean résumé.

Because the world doesn't ask
what held you down.

It doesn't slow down.
It doesn't rewind.
It doesn't care.

It just keeps moving—
and dares you to explain
why you didn't.

THE PASSENGER

The window fogs before the rain begins.
Like my body knows what's coming
before I let it in.

I'm always in the passenger seat these days—
of cars, of lives,
of conversations where I nod
just to keep from vanishing.

The glass blurs. The city softens.
And I watch it all unfold
as if I'm outside myself...
a ghost with warm hands,
sitting in a car
that no one's waiting to get into.

I've cried here before.
Not loud.
Not enough to make a scene.
Just the kind of crying
that fogs the glass from the inside,
and leaves a stain
only I can see.

You learn a lot about pain
when you feel it quietly,
how it has seasons.

How it grows polite.
How it waits
until the music stops
to settle into the silence beside you.

There are fingerprints on the window
from where I've tried to make shapes—
some small reminder I was here.
But they fade. Always.
Like everything else I couldn't hold.

People love a broken story
when it ends in redemption.
They want the rain to mean something.
They want me to find the sun again.
To tell them this was just the middle.

But what if it's not?

What if this is it?
The part of the road
where no one comes looking?

What if I'm the "before" picture
they scroll past,
a still frame of someone
still breathing
but long erased
from the reel of other people's lives?

They knock sometimes—
well-meaning hands
rapping on the glass,
saying *come out,*
as if the door isn't rusted shut.

As if this isn't the only place
I still recognize myself.

I want to scream.
Not for help.
Just for the record.

To say I was here—
that I weathered a life
inside this rolling tomb
of rain-soaked silence.

But the storm outside
knows my name too well.
And every time I try to speak,
the windows just fog again.

And I remain, passenger and witness,
watching the world blur past me
like it has always done.

Archivist Notes:

"Heaven closed its curtains.
So, we wrote our own damn play.
The saints went silent,
their hymns, tucked away.

But sin, darling?
Sin was always center stage.
Velvet-voiced, red-lipped,
wild, untamed, unphased.

So, take your script—
the show's begun.
Which sin will you pick
when the lights find ***you***
alone in Act One?"

"Of Sinners And Sin"

ROOM No.: 5
Observer Type: For the Tempters
Status: Red Sealed
Memory Type: Moral Transcripts
Lighting Condition: Stage Lights; Shadows
Compiled By: The Archivist
Date Restored: [redacted]

ACT I

THE MIRROR AND THE CROWN

[The curtain rises on PRIDE. Enter SUPERBIA]

They named me "son of fire and glass,"
Born where no humble foot could pass.
Before the light, before decree,
There was no king until I said ***"me."***

The sins all gathered, drawn to see,
Which one of them could rival me.
They knelt before my gilded glare,
The wretched whispering: *"All hail the heir!"*

I poured chaos into grace with one whisper in,
And I taught the saints the taste of sin.
Cast me down? Then rise and burn,
Let sins with spines await their turn.

I drank from pools of pure applause,
Each cheer a law, each gaze a clause.
What need had I for mortal plea?
I am the storm. The crown. The sea.

They call me sin? I call it spark.
The flame that dared to kiss the dark.
You named it vanity, a crime.
I named it truth. So did time.

Still, they begged, *"Step down. Descend!"*
But how does Heaven condescend?
What king steps down to blend with kin?
To bow would be the greatest sin.

Yet if I fall— I fall in gold.
For I am Pride, the fierce and bold
And even other sins bow low
Each time they feel my shadow grow

Did you not build cathedrals
Just to mirror how I gleam?
Crowned your kings and called it honor,
All to worship just a dream?

You pray for grace?
I forged that path.
You kneel to virtue?
I lured her to wrath.

You call this a reckoning?

Child, *please sit.*
I've worn crowns
heavier than your wit.

So, raise up your gavel, deliver your verse.
Call me your sin, your triumph, your curse.
But history listens, and time always sees—
That kingdoms still crawl
At the crease of my knees.

[Exit SUPERBIA, adjusting his collar]

ACT II

ON MY KNEES, AMEN

[Enter LUXURIA]

I wear sin like whispered lace,
Soft at the hips, wild in the face.
With lacquered lips and need that steals,
I walk like thirst that wears her heels.

I speak in shivers down the spine,
In moans between the holy line.
I pull, I press, I stain, I slide,
The sin that lingers on your pride.

I waltz in glances, wet and wide,
A gaze that parts what vows would hide.
I walk in heat, I breathe in ache,
I'm every vow you'll swear, then break.

My hands wear silk, my tongue wears lies,
I touch, and hymns dissolve in sighs.
I sip from lips, I bite in prayer,
And leave your virtues stripped and bare.

Halos slip like ties undone,
By fingers fluent in the fun.

An ache for more, their throats sing,
To every pulse and pulsing thing.

I bloom in beds where names dissolve,
Where rings come off and wrists absolve
I drink from throats still wet with prayer,
I kiss the guilt and keep it there.

I've danced through kings with open doors,
And left them clawing at their wars.
You call it fall, I call it flight,
The ecstasy of wrong made right.

I pull no chains, yet men are leashed.
I give them a thirst that's never eased.
The mouth may plead, the spine may twist,
But none forget the way I kissed.

I crowned myself with bitten gold,
And every moan I've ever sold.
You preach of purity and fate?
Then why do you look and *salivate?*

Let brides clutch veils and grooms seek grace,
When I am worship face to face.
No shame, no guilt, no final bell,
You know my name. You wear it well.

Come, let your prayers lose their fire—
Whisper me, dove, your last desire.
For I am want, your velvet plea,
Salvation has never tasted like me.

[Exit LUXURIA, lipstick smudged]

ACT III

THE SECOND SERPENT

[Enter INVIDIA, eyes locked on SUPERBIA's crown]

I smiled the night they crowned you king,
Then bit the hand that kissed your ring.
I am the green between your gold.
I am a story, centuries old.

A serpent learns to shed a skin,
To lie in wait with coiled-up grin,
To know that time is half the fight,
Before he learns to how to strike.

There is a difference between desire and me,
If it's not mine, then let it cease to be.
I'd break the crown, snap every stem,
If I can't wear the gold of them.

Blessed are the adorned, they said.
Blessed are the crowned and fed.
But I drank storm from cracks in altar stone,
And claimed that hollowed seat alone.

But I learned your laugh, I stole your grace,
I mimicked the softness in your face.
Each mirror found me— almost you,
A little wrong. A little true.

Your lovers looked at me too long.
Your poems bled into my song.
So, I slip, echo, wear your skin,
And take the praise I couldn't win.

I took your jokes and made them sing,
I bowed before your every spring.
I wore your name in quieter rooms,
And fed the envy where it blooms.

And still you smiled— soft, unaware,
I played the ghost inside your glare.
Your eyes like windows I could haunt,
I feed myself on what you flaunt.

I don't bite unless you call,
And you were halfway to a fall.
You left the door just slightly bare,
So I made myself a home in there.

I'm the evil one, you say?
I'm the one who led you astray?
Yet with every choice, you carved your way.
Look harder in the mirror today.

So, tell me, love, wasn't that your thought,
The 'want' you wore, the praise you sought?
Or I'm the one whispered through your sleep?
Whose hunger taught your heart to creep?

You bite your tongue, but why, my dear?
What truth draws close that stings your ear?
Is that restraint—or fear of me?
Or is it the guilt you will not see?

I live in glances, side-long, slight.
In scrolls, in silence, in pretend.

You hate the ones who dim your light
Because I taught you not to bend.

Do tell me dear and
Tell me ***true:***
Haven't you ever clapped
With clenched fists too?

Smiled through teeth
As they praised another?
Loved your friend...
But watched their lover?

Have you not traced their joy with your eyes,
Tried on their triumph in your guise?
And just for a moment— ***admit***— you fit?
Didn't that sweetness almost commit?

Have you never prayed
For your idol to fail,
Or dreamed your rival
Pale and frail?

Don't lie.
I caught the twitch beneath your praise.
The shadow curled in candle blaze.
The hunger you disguise as grace.
You and I, we share a face.

[Exit INVIDIA, slithering behind the throne]

ACT IV

THE SLEEPER'S OATH

[Enter ACEDIA, late to his own act]

Come lie with me, beneath the sun,
Where hours melt and time's undone.
"The world can wait," you softly sigh,
"Dreams make finer friends than try."

Why chase the wind? It never stays.
Why bleed for someone else's praise?
Let others burn, I'll hush the ache,
And give you all you long to take.

Don't mind the crumbs, the unwashed cup,
The half-seen tasks you gave up.
If silence grows, if stillness wins,
What's lost in sleep is the softest sin.

Let others sweat for goals and names,
Let others climb their noisy flames.
But you—you bloom when you are still.
The climb was never worth the hill.

I offer you a gentler cage,
With velvet walls to dull your rage.

No pain, no loss, no flame, no climb...
Just perfect peace, and stolen time.

Thus, each dream delayed became a stone,
Each "not today" was set in bone.
You said, *"Tomorrow."* I hummed, *"Sure."*
And every door stayed shut one day more.

You let the calls go unanswered.
You let the bread mold in the bag.
You let the messages rot unopened,
because answering means *beginning,*
and beginning means *moving,*
and moving means *caring,*
and isn't it easier not to?

You used to scream for more than this,
But rest rewrote what hunger is.
A little break became a wall,
A softer voice, a longer fall.

You grew too tired to lift your name,
Too slow to stoke your former flame.
The sky still shone a distant peak,
Too far for arms grown slow and weak.

So, tell me *truly,* do I seem strange?
Or do you know my quiet range?
The tug that keeps your limbs in bed,
The velvet fog inside your head?

Was it not I who kissed your brow
Each time you said, "Just not right now"?
I rocked you sweet when day was bright,
Then pulled you softly out of sight.

Have you not stalled the waking morn,

Hit snooze on life you once had sworn?
Rolled over, rejected the tiring pace,
Choosing the dreams to dodge the race?

Is that your back on soft sheets pressed,
Or will surrendered, unconfessed?
Is that your voice gone still, and why?
Too tired to rise, too numb to try?

I do not haunt, I don't demand,
I simply take what leaves your hand.
The half-built dreams, the plans gone cold,
I keep them all. I let them mold.

Do you recall the thrill you knew?
What happened to the flame in you?
Do tell me true and tell me right:
Do you still feel your former light?

You call me sin, but dressed me nice,
You kissed my lips of lotus ice.
You built a shrine of softness, yes,
Then laid inside its sweet recess.

So, hush. I know your tired heart.
You always sigh before you start.
Stay. No dawn. No test. No crest.
Just fold into me—
Rest,
like moss on stone.
Rest,
like dusk undone.
Rest,
till even memory forgets the sun.

[Exit ACEDIA, yawning]

ACT V

THE HUNGERING KIND

[Enter GULA]

Ladies and gents, your plates are bare.
But don't you fret, I've got your share.
Oh, don't get shy, you are part of the show.
You fed me more than you'll ever know.

"No?" you say?
Mmm. Yes. That tastes like denial, soft decay.
Delicate. I like it over-seasoned.
Pairs well with guilt dressed as reason.

But I, my sweet, I know your cost.
You eat the thing you fear you've lost.
I was raised on buttered breath,
Fed on fruit too sweet to last,
On flesh too soft, desires cast
Like coins into an endless pit.
What did I do?
I swallowed it.

I sip from praise, I bite applause,
I crave it raw, without a cause.

My tongue recalls each name it knew—

Abundance. Riches. Something new.
I gnawed on dreams with ivory skin,
Bit kingdoms down from deep within.
I bit through love mid-sugared line,
And licked its lacquered edge like wine.

Glory? *I sucked its marrow dry.*
Pity? *Salted, stacked, and high.*
Hope? *A chewy, rubber treat—*
Digestible with wine and deceit.

Grief? Oh, yes. *I like it aged.*
Soft and slow, despair encaged.
Marinated. Salted right.
Best served in the sleepless night.

I am the beast beneath your grins,
The first to crawl to the last of sins.
Where others taste, I take. I take.
I chew through joy for hunger's sake.

I am the bite that follows thrill,
The extra sip that breaks the will,
The ache that purrs beneath your skin,
You hush it once, then let it in.

I've eaten beauty past its prime,
Wrinkled sweet, and soaked in time.
You wanted more? I served it hot.
And—look how much you've got.

You let me in with every bite,
Each *"just one more"* at dead of night.
I drank your time in golden sips,
Then sucked the sugar off your lips.
You loved it, didn't you? The glow?
The way I made your empties grow?

I whispered: *"More."* You said: *"Just one."*
And now your feast is far from done.

The meal is you. The need. The ache.
The breath you hold, the choice you fake.
Then you swore, *"No more!"* then reached again.
Gluttony knows the ripest *"when."*

So, what if you need a second slice?
Is your will so weak, few bites suffice?

Now, remember that midnight binge?
Not of food—no, no—
Of watching, wanting, wishing,
Until your eyes burned blue,
And your mind turned to syrup.
I lapped it up—your silvered screen,
The hollow hush, the dopamine.

You thought you could handle it, didn't you?
A little indulgence. A nibble of excess.
But hunger blooms when fed too deep,
And bites the hand it wants to keep.

The last course served is always you.
The void left when I am through.
And once I'm full, you'll finally see:
I feasted on who you used to be.

[Exit GULA, still reaching]

ACT VI

THE GOSPEL OF FLAME

[Enter IRA]

I arrived fists-first,
red-palmed,
a tantrum wearing skin.
The first fury, *marked on one,*
the eldest sin, the shadowed son.

When anvil sings, the forge gives birth,
When flames rewrite the gospel's worth,
Ragged lungs still forge the fire,
Wrath is wrought in molten wire...

I am what happens
when mercy chokes
on its own tongue,
when silence splits
and the quiet comes undone.

Strike after strike, the sparks would rise,
A thousand suns in a hundred skies.

Whose name do you press like a bruise in your mouth?
How many apologies drowned in the drought,
fossilized into fury you can't spit out?

You rehearse forgiveness
like a eulogy for the living,
let rot fester where your fire should singe.

Fool, I say.

They told you: *breathe.*
I told you: ***scream.***
They said: *let it go.*
I said: ***don't you dare, no.***

The snarl in your gut
when they cut you off again?
The flame in your eyes
when they laugh,
as if you weren't burning within?

I saw it—
that grin.
You stretched it so wide
your gums split thin,
a smile sharpened to sin.
First brother of blood, first heir of the blade,
your smile knows the soil where a shadow was laid.

Oh, admit it:
rage fits you best.
A gun for your sorrow,
a scourge for the rest.

Look at you now,
smoke in your throat,

truth blistering your tongue.
Don't swallow it.
Go on.
Lift your voice.
Smite their laughter.
Split their lies.
If the world won't listen,
then let it ***ignite.***

  Stay meek, *stay chained?*
Or wear me instead—
the flame in your chest,
the scripture in red.

[Exit IRA, smoke trailing behind him]

ACT VII

OPULENCE, DARLING

[Enter AVARITIA, other sins lurking behind]

I was born with a silver spoon,
and bit straight through it.

Gold flakes in my cereal,
crushed velvet in my crib.
I learned early: enough is a lie,
why settle for less
when every treasure calls your eye?

I want it all: ring, finger, crown, orchard bright,
All that glimmers tempts my sight.
Even silence—I demand it louder,
Even praise—I flaunt it prouder.

Don't look away; you've tasted the thrill of more,
Lingering over treasures not your own,
Devouring with your eyes,
Coveting with your silence,
That second helping of attention,
The praise you didn't need, but took anyway.

You say you want "just enough,"
But I see the tremble in your fingers
When "enough" walks by

In heels sharper than your self-control.

You hoard kindness like currency,
give only to get.
If even generosity wears gold-threaded strings—why share?

I like you this way.
Hungry. Wanting.
A mouth slightly parted,
a hunger draped in pearls.
Let others play saints.

You were born with ribboned lies on your tongue,
a craving for more in your bloodstream.
I see the drool,
hear the soft gnawing in your bones
that whispers: *more, more, more,*
even when your hands are full.

I warned you, didn't I?
That wanting me
meant you'd never stop.

Tell me,
how many compliments
did you collect today
just to keep yourself warm?
How many people
do you love only when they look expensive?

Do you *feel it,* children of appetite?
With every glance, every bite, every night?
Let every longing feed your thirst.
Mark this:
The world will crown the covetous first.

Hear now the sins awaken at my call,
Brightest wings now condemned to fall.

I sit with wrath, with lust I dine,
Envied treasures, with sloth divine.
Gluttony gnaws, pride preens its thread,
All sins kneel where my hunger is fed.

Bow, mortals, bow, for I am the last call,
The sum of desires, the want of them all.

[Exit AVARITIA, ALL recede as curtain falls]

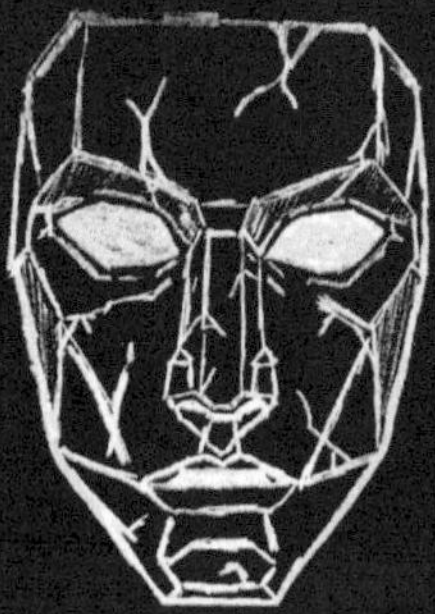

Archivist Notes:

"Step off the maps you've ever been,
You must wear the mask to be seen.
Draw the circle, speak it true,
The trade begins in three... two..."

"Whispers From Oldhaven"

ROOM No.: 6
Observer Type: For the Seekers
Status: Special Permit Only; Mask Required
Memory Type: Classified Records
Lighting Condition: Nyxite-lit
Compiled By: The Archivist
Date Restored: [redacted]

THE DEBT BELOW

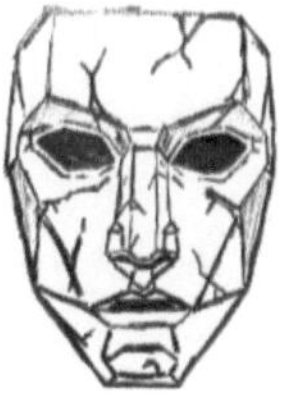

Carved into tunnel wall,
[Gate Mirevale, Undergrid]

Stones remember every deal
so dare not cheat, dare not steal.

Trade a trinket for a piece of dream,
and dream you get... or a buried scream.

What you give is more than shown;
some trades are made with flesh and bone.

They'll sell you light, they'll sell you flame,
but some have left without their name.

The stone remembers. It keeps the debt.
It hums for all who can't forget.

So, speak your price, but guard your plea,
not all you trade is ever free.

So, if you bid, bid with fear.
The market hears.
The market hears.

ENTRY 477-A

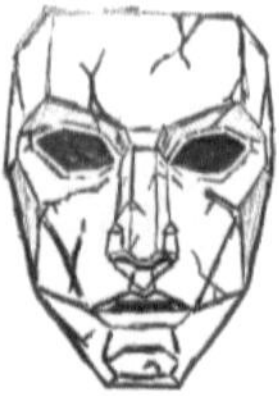

Council Record Excerpt - Security Breach
[Gate Lirrah, Undergrid]

A mask was worn by a different face.
A name was spoken none could trace.
The circle drawn— too smooth, too sure
The gate gave way; no warded cure.

No new trader marked a deal that night.
No coin was cast, no new barter right.
Yet Nyxite in the southern vein
Fell still for three, then thrice again.

The hum returned at 03:03.
But silence tolls what none can see.
One voice recalled: a child, quite pale
"She was small. She carried a mail."

By *Vote of Nine,* in stone inscribed,
The rite shall change. The locks revised.
A phrase of seal shall now be said:
"Vel'toren niven drassa ved."

Let no heirloom mask suffice.
The old blood shall not pay the price.

WHAT TIME STOLE BACK

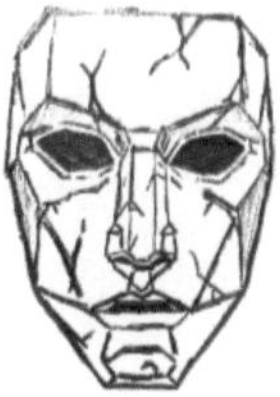

Filed Entry – Old Haven Council Archives

Subject: Marek (Undergrid Origin)
Cell: No. 7, Eastern Bastion
Status: Deceased
Item Recovered: Letter (Unsent)
Class: Trade Violation – Time Magic, Unauthorized

Dear Seriane,

I know this will not find you in light,
so let it find you in legend.
Or perhaps it will never find anyone at all.
But I write to remember— to cage what little time remains.

The days with you were never short,
yet I bartered eternity for hours.
How cheap I made it seem:
the curve of your laugh, the warmth of your breath
shared beneath borrowed stars.

I bought flame, and fed it our names.
If you wondered why, you grew tired so soon,
why your hands grew colder with every return,

I pray you never knew.
I pray your last thought was not of me.

I never learned how to stop wanting you.
Even when I should have.
Even when the toll began.

You laughed less.
Slept more.
And I—
I watched, and did not tell.
I let the hours slip from your skin,
because I could not bear to miss a single second more.

It was not meant to end this way.

They locked me away not only for the trade,
but for the sin of knowing and choosing it anyway.

They warned me,
those who sell in whispers, cloaked in dusk:
That time bought is time twisted.
But love made me reckless,
and words made it worse.

All I said was, make her time mine.
I wished to share, not steal.
But hunger listens differently than intent,
and magic keeps the ledger that mortals cannot.
So, it took what I could not give back.
One breath at a time.

The Market took more than I paid for.
Your breath shortened, your eyes dimmed.
And still I let you come.

What I bought was not our eternity, Seriane,

it was the end, feathered and soft,
disguised as a gift.

Now, I write from the cell.
Now the walls hum with absence.
Now my nights stretch long, touched by price.
They call it exile. I call it penance.
The ink barely clings,
but I must say it:
I'm sorry.
For stealing from your days.
For holding you tighter than time would allow.

—M

[[redacted] | ORIGIN: OL_HVN_-A]

Traced to a vault *beneath* Room 6.

...

3 excerpts deemed unstable.

...

Awaiting full recovery…

...

– From the chronicles of a world, you've yet to meet.
Coming soon.

...

<< ARCHIVE SESSION TERMINATED >>

FILE SEALED BY: **THE ARCHIVIST**

ACKNOWLEDGMENTS

To my mother — the heartbeat behind every page.
You never let me give up on this, even when I almost did.
Your belief built the spine of this book.

To my father — who's held space for every version of me,
long before I ever knew what I wanted to become.

To my brother — who never once said "no,"
no matter how wild the dream.
Thank you for making the impossible feel within reach.

And to you, the reader — thank you for arriving.
For turning these pages with care.
For meeting my almosts with your own.
This book is ours now.

WHY "ALMOSTS"?

Because "almost" is the truest measure of being human.
Most of us don't live in absolutes.
We live more often at thresholds than at triumphs.

Almosts are not failures.
They are small, unfinished threads,
but they pull at us all the same.
They ache, they shimmer, they haunt.
And in their incompleteness,
they remind us that we once reached.
That we wanted.
That we tried.

To keep them is an act of reverence.
To name them is an act of courage.
And to archive them—
is to admit that incompletion
has its own kind of immortality.

This book was not a catalogue of endings,
but of doorways left ajar.
Here dwelled the fragments,
the unfinished loves.
the half-healed wounds,
the unsent letters.

And I am their keeper.
Their archivist.
And in preserving them,
I preserve us—
all the selves **we were,**
all the selves **we almost became.**

MEET THE ARCHIVIST

I believe every object holds a story,
and every observer holds a key.

I am a seeker of such stories tucked inside forgotten things—an old journal abandoned at a train station, a button lost beneath floorboards, an object carrying the weight of a hundred hands. I write to understand the ghosts I carry, and the ones I meet along the way.

This book was born in a season of loss,
when I felt unmoored and directionless.
Writing became both compass and companion,
guiding me back to myself.

I write in fragments and freefall, in rhymes that sometimes forget to rhyme, in verses that lean toward grief, mystery, and myth. When I am not writing, I am rereading lines that already know me, or watching the sky as if it might finally answer back.

I grew up in Kolkata, India.
With a degree in biotechnology and a poet's pulse,
I live between two languages of wonder—
where science measures what is,
and story reaches for what might be.

This is my first book.
If you are holding it now, thank you.
And if these pages have stirred something in you,
then the objects and stories I've followed
have found their way home.

— Natasha Rahman Khan

www.ingramcontent.com/pod-product-compliance
Ingram Content Group UK Ltd.
Pitfield, Milton Keynes, MK11 3LW, UK
UKHW040036200726
13845UKWH00054B/414

9 789334 422450